# Smudges

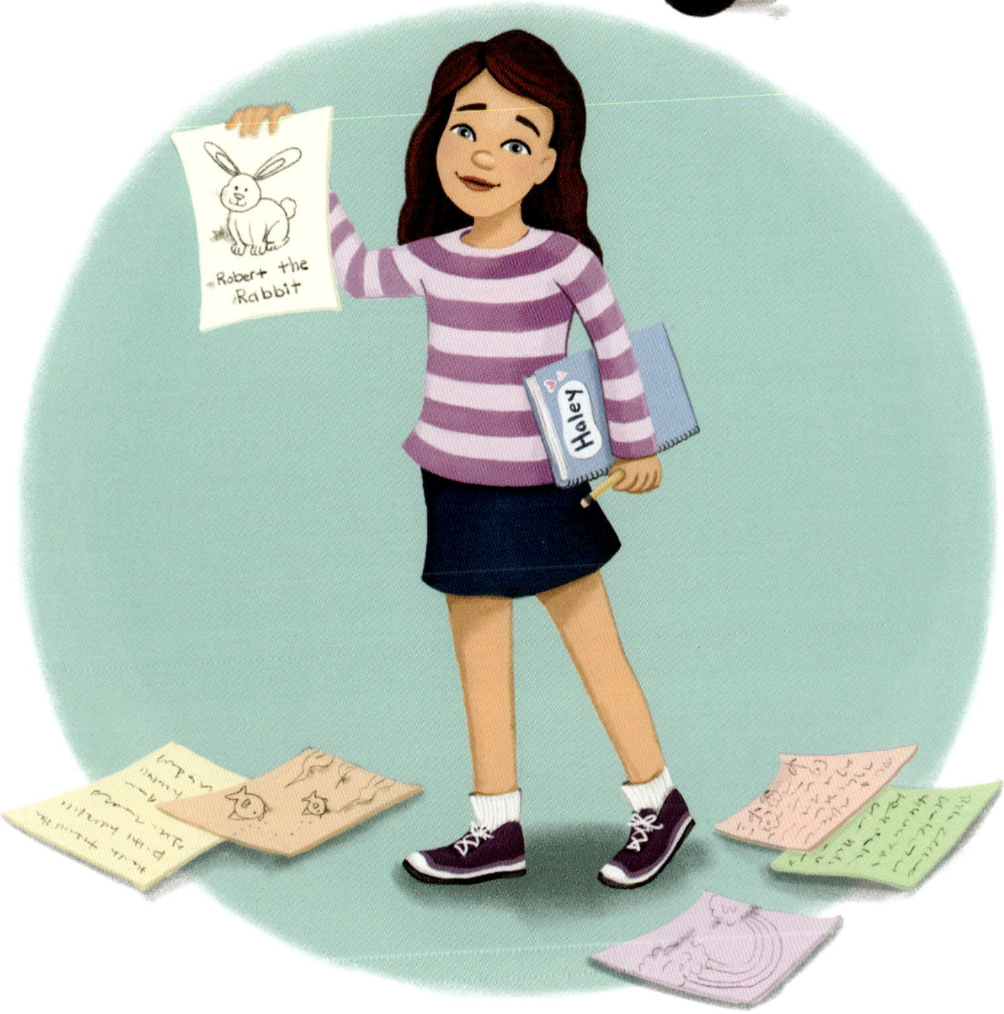

Lauren Emerson

Illustrated by Kim Soderberg

© 2024 Lauren Emerson

All rights reserved. No part of this book may be used or reproduced in any manner without written permission except in the case of brief quotations embodied in critical articles or reviews.

This is a work of fiction. Any similarity to real persons, living or dead, is coincidental and not intended by the author.

*Smudges*

Brown Books Kids
Dallas / New York
www.BrownBooksKids.com
(972) 381-0009

A New Era in Publishing®

Publisher's Cataloging-In-Publication Data

Names: Emerson, Lauren, author. | Soderberg, Kimberly, illustrator.
Title: Smudges / Lauren Emerson ; illustrated by Kim Soderberg.
Description: Dallas ; New York : Brown Books Kids, [2024] | Audience: Juvenile. | Summary: When Mr. Hart asks his class to think of something that makes each of them unique, Haley is stumped. Everyone else, it seems, has at least one quality or skill that makes them stand out. But what does Haley have?--Publisher.
Identifiers: ISBN: 978-1-61254-673-5 (hardcover) | LCCN: 2023949672
Subjects: LCSH: Individual differences--Juvenile fiction. | Students--Juvenile fiction. | Ability--Juvenile fiction. | Characters and characteristics--Juvenile fiction. | Self-esteem--Juvenile fiction. | CYAC: Individual differences--Fiction. | Students--Fiction. | Ability--Fiction. | Characters and characteristics--Fiction. | Self-esteem--Fiction. | BISAC: JUVENILE FICTION / Social Themes / Self-Esteem & Self-Reliance. | JUVENILE FICTION / Social Themes / New Experience.
Classification: LCC: PZ7.1.E4736 Sm 2024 | DDC: [E]--dc23

This book has been officially leveled by using the F&P Text Level Gradient™ Leveling System.

ISBN 978-1-61254-673-5
LCCN 2023949672

Printed in China
10 9 8 7 6 5 4 3 2 1

For more information or to contact the author, please go to www.LaurenEmersonBooks.com.

## DEDICATION

For Elle and Owen

## ACKNOWLEDGEMENTS

This book was inspired by my students and our classroom community. I'm always in awe of their open hearts and minds. When we celebrate what makes us unique, it brings us together and makes us stronger—just like the pieces of a puzzle.

Haley loved to write. She never ran out of ideas. Each blank page was the start of a new adventure.

Sometimes she would doodle.

Other times she would write jokes.

And sometimes she would write stories from her vivid imagination.

The only things Haley didn't love about writing were the pencil smudges that covered her hand.

Her paper got messy too.

## Ugh!

**This always happens,**
she thought.

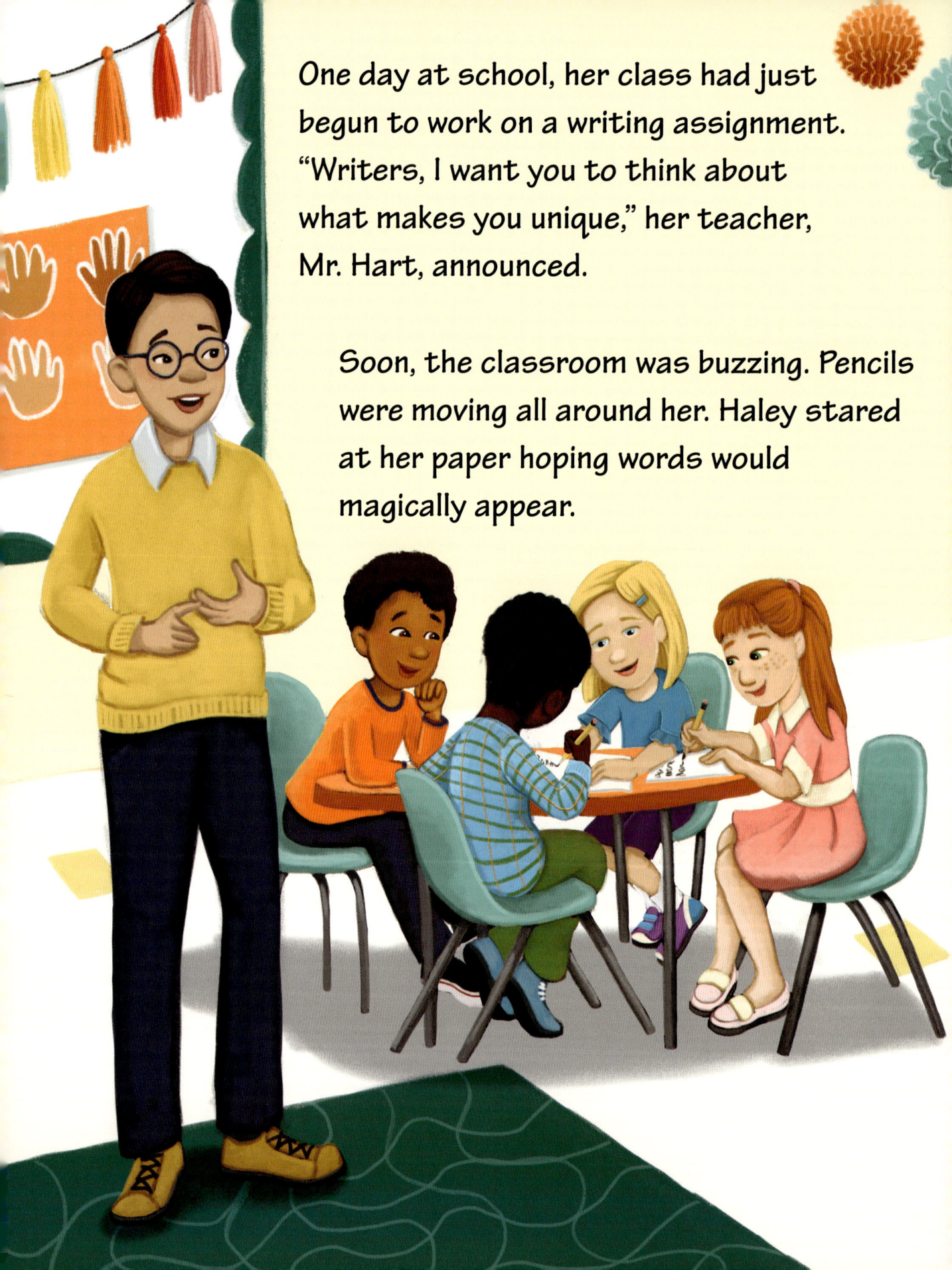

One day at school, her class had just begun to work on a writing assignment. "Writers, I want you to think about what makes you unique," her teacher, Mr. Hart, announced.

Soon, the classroom was buzzing. Pencils were moving all around her. Haley stared at her paper hoping words would magically appear.

For the first time ever, she couldn't think of anything to write. She ripped the empty page out of her notebook and crumpled it up.

After recess, Mr. Hart held up a blank puzzle piece. He explained that each student would cut one out and decorate it to go with their writing assignment. "At the end of our unit, we'll celebrate by sharing what makes each of you unique."

Soon, art supplies were sprinkled all over their desks, but Haley couldn't find her scissors.

"Here, you can use mine," Mateo offered.

"Oh thanks, but my scissors make it easier for me to cut. I'll keep looking." Haley felt her face turn red as she sank down as far as she could in her seat.

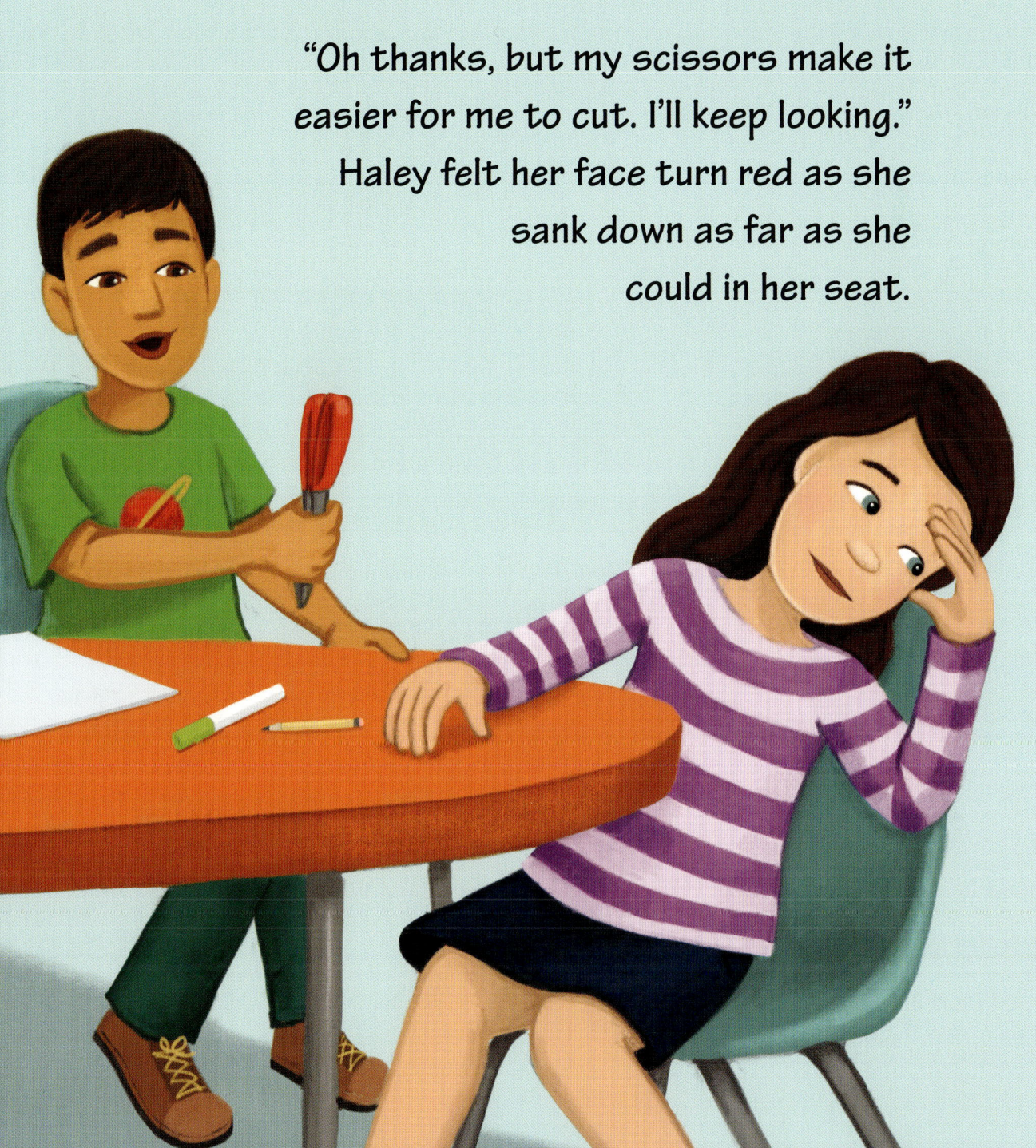

During work time, Haley showed Mr. Hart her empty notebook. "Don't worry! There's something unique about each of us." He smiled and encouraged her to talk with her classmates.

What makes you unique?

#Kindness   #1 Teacher

Ava spoke up first. "I'm writing about my colorful glasses!" she exclaimed. Haley wished she wore something special.

Mateo was decorating his puzzle piece in English and Spanish.

"I'm bilingual . . . that means I can speak two languages," he explained. Haley wished she had a skill like that.

Haley opened her notebook and tapped her pencil. Nothing. She could feel the tears starting to blur in her eyes, but she knew she had to keep trying.

*Maybe drawing about it will help?* she thought.

As she was drawing, Ava leaned over to admire Haley's work.

"Wow! That looks so cool. Can you show me how to do that?" she said.

Maybe my smudges aren't so bad, Haley thought.

Now it was Haley's turn to meet with Mr. Hart. "How's it going?" he asked.

"I still can't think of what makes me unique," sighed Haley.

"Sometimes writers just need time to think. Take a break. You never know where you might find some inspiration," said Mr. Hart.

Later that day, Mr. Hart started to read aloud to the class. Haley closed her eyes as the characters swirled in her head. When she opened them, she glanced down at the pencil marks on her hand.

As she started to wipe them off,
a smile slowly spread across her face.
She finally knew what made her unique.
It had been there all along.

On the day of their author celebration, Haley felt butterflies dancing in her stomach. "OK class, it's time for each of you to shine!" Mr. Hart exclaimed.

One by one, her classmates shared what made them unique, and their class puzzle grew.

"I'm a twin," said Marcus.

"I have red hair," said Grace.

"My family is from Nigeria," said Obi.

"I have a birthmark," said Isabel.

But there was still one puzzle piece missing up on the wall. Haley's classmates twisted and turned in their seats.

Who did the last piece belong to?
Who hadn't shared yet?

What makes you unique?

It was Haley's turn. She walked to the front of the room and proudly held up her hand with silvery pencil marks.

"I'm unique because I'm left-handed!" Haley explained. "Lefties do some things differently. But that makes us creative problem solvers!"

"In school I use special scissors."

"At home I have my own measuring cup."

"And I wear a left-handed glove when I play catch with my friends."

With Haley's piece in place, their puzzle was complete, and the class cheered.

The following week, Haley's class started to work on a new writing assignment.

"Writers, I want you to think about something you could teach the class," said Mr. Hart.

This time, Haley couldn't wait to get started. In fact, she knew just what to write about.

The best part?

Her smudges were finally going to come in handy!

# DISCUSSION ACTIVITY

### Before reading:
- Discuss the word *unique*.
- Describe a time you felt stuck as a writer. How did it feel? What helped you?

### During reading:
- What are some of Haley's character traits?
- What *does* Haley try when she is stuck as a writer?

### After reading:
- Why were the smudges on Haley's hand important to the story?
- How can we be unique on the inside and the outside?
- Why is it important to share what makes us unique?
- How can our differences make us stronger?
- What lessons did Haley learn in the story?
- Decorate and share your own puzzle piece! Template available on LaurenEmersonBooks.com.

What makes you unique?